Embrace The Tribe

by Tango Winnie Idjabe Makuale

Cover illustration by Laia Makuale

For Abaipe.

PART ONE

From the waves of the diaspora.

From the waves of the diaspora,
and a migrant's staggering.

From my "badass" days
and the "I'm truly done" ones.

With an unknown accent,
and a loud heartbeat,

and a bunch of tools
to destroy few demons.

For those who feel broken
after all the battles lost

and put together all the pieces,
owning their times.

For those who are warriors
without a place to call home

fighting for breath peaceful
counterclockwise.

For those who dispatch prayers
in the name of a beloved god

feeding gently the incorporeal
come rain or shine.

For the mamas and the students,
and the activists and the ramblers,
and the mediators and the witches.

Celebrating that we conquer.
Celebrating that we're here.
Celebrating that we're brave.

The person you become.

The person you become when you speak more than
one language is the result of experiences,
culture and seeds.

The beauty of be able to communicate,
to connect with different realities,
to access to knowledge.

Hidden opportunities appear in their best version
and new challenges ask you for a date.

Your soul join fresh ways to empowerment,
your mind grow bigger, grow free.

She likes to read with coconut oil in her fingerprints.

She likes to read with coconut oil in her fingerprints,
just after fix her crown.
Her treasures follow the rhythm of last Nelson Freitas
song.

Sometimes she stays in a page for minutes, smiling.
And jumps the last sentence of the prose.

When her mama comes from home, real pineapples
join her readings.
When her mama is abroad, she is flanked by spirits.

They protect her as her gods,
sewing the holes that life gave her,
living the marks as a reminder.

So If her memory ever pack its stuffs,
she just has to kindly touch her hands
to feel safe in her own body.

She belongs to her ancestors.

She belongs to her ancestors,
and her rhythms and her blues.
And bissap and some "fufú".
She belongs to her ancestors,
and her combs and her books.
And the rain and the moon.
And her manners and her moves.
And her people and her roots.
Going to pray all afternoons.
Everyday is a thanksgiving,
well, she says so.
Puts the prefix before the number,
every time she calls.

We are alive.
We are alive, after all this time.
After all the storms on our people heads.
Doing balances between our mental health
and our personal growth.
Dealing setbacks and unfriendly memories.
Seeing how they are killing us
slowly, smoothly, heartless.
Waking up early to assurance a plate,
for our children, for our bellies.
Inhaling news that sometimes ain't grateful.
Breathing. Chin up.
We are alive.

Your speech is valid.
The revolution have been always here, dear.
And so, your speech is valid.
Doesn't matter where is coming from.

Speak from the anger is as workable as speak from a
peacemaker vocal cord.
The aim of make a change comes in many shapes.

As murders are called accident depending on who is
the actor and persecutions are still trending in the
neighborhood.

As cross the frontier to the promise golden is
dangerous but there are free passport to go to our
islands.

Advertisements judge and label ethnic groups while
Carnival is celebrated doing blackface.

And we are not for sale,
"I am sick and tired" a woman said
in front of Libya's Embassy.

Temples of worship should be a safe space.
And people do not act in the wake of their religious
beliefs, they are individuals,
generalize is so unfair.

African children privacy is a must:
for those who shoot for their Tinder's CV and for those
who report it through screenshots in their Instagram.

And those children do deserve to blossom with their dadas at home, not in cells due to injustices.

As they do not deserve to be afraid in the streets while society don't care about the origin of the knives.

While society don't care about temporary houses becoming a long term nightmare.

There are people out there who live outside the demonstration slogans,
outside the protest signs.

And maybe you got something to say about all this, and your speech is valid, and I'm here to hear.

Red sand

Red sand,
mango trees,
yellows and greens,
forty degrees,
bags of water,
hot tea,
kora players,
Yaa Asantewaa.

Marching to the sun,
hit twice the pickup.

Emotions.

You got the right to be scared.
You got the right to feel tired.
You got the right to stay in bed.
You got the right to make mistakes.

It's okay to cry.
It's okay to scramble.
It's okay to cancel plans.
It's okay to be mad.

Let yourself to turn off the phone.
Let yourself to introduce the emotions.
Let yourself to change your mind.
Let yourself to restart.

You are your priority.

Boiling water
Boiling water in the kettle,
socks caught up in XPression.

The new couple is dancing until the shoulder and the
room smells like Vicks Vaporub.

We are sistas

We are sistas from a different land,
struggled against the apart hood,
lifting the same pure water.

I would love to hold your hand,
speak out about our truth.
Embrace the tribe with you.

Sequences have been deleted,
but is never too late
to note the baked paths

We receive blessing in our mother tongue,
Miriam Makeba is singing.
Home is where is the Aba'A.

Kaolin clay grinding,
outside is lightly raining,
plantains are already fried.

Remember our elderly speaking
their knowledge is power to us,
reunite the culture back.

PART TWO

Resilience

Having a talk with myself I wonder:
Am I alrightie, am I safe?
From the earth and all the pain.
Are you coming? Can you stay?
Running flawless, always late.

Miss your movements and your breath
Sleeping, my angel, next to me.
All the adventures that you've lived.
With the joyful that you bring.
All the dances that you rocked
Are stuck in just one word.

And down here, in this world
People keep showing their glow.
And babes, I'm doing.
Not good, not bad. Just doing.
There are weeks that I'm blooming.
And others that I am.
I am.

Holding my own back
pretending that is easy.

Trusting in my good luck
Leaving the grief to energies.

Well, I need you so bad
Can't hide this feel for ages

No fuss, no rush. But
hermana, come and heal me.

My tuition fee was declined.

Twice.
Apparently you don't deserve it when you have studied high education before.
Apparently no one let you know in advance.

It's painful, when life don't give you second chances.
I haven't finished my last undergraduate, I was focus playing hide and seek with my previous landlady.
And it was easy because I had no electricity every two months.
Since then, bills included, always.

Leaving uni was hard because this group of black girls, trust me, are magic.
Magic as my French teacher,
magic as his see you soon words.
Leaving uni was hard because I wanted to call Foday uncle.
Because he is dark and soft.
And talkative and warm.
Leaving uni was hard because I'm working just next to and I'm not gutsy enough to stop by and say hi to that lovely Catalan student.

Happy days are yet to come. They better.
I'm going to surprise myself with some yellow flowers.
If I let them lay down on my bed before the first Sambuca,
tomorrow's me won't believe how much someone care about her tonight.

Half an hour ain't enough
to kick away my ghosts,
my fears and my doubts,
keep designing my goals.

So I slept two hours.
Two hours and a half.

Sunflower
Sunflowers won't shine this winter
the weather is not being fair.

Their own light gonna come brighter:
a breakdown is not an end.

Don't mess around a fighter,
they need their own space.

Don't force them to grow quicker
because you want to smell.

Sunflowers need some water,
sunflowers need a break.

Feel me, full me, fill me.

I love the weather
I love the weather between your blankets,
the loud of your whispers,
your dark skin.

Your braids wrap up my bones,
warm up my fears,
wash up my aches.

Move one step closer,
I'll water you every single morning.

Last poem
I barely recognize the woman in the mirror, but the
cheekbones, an unknown family tree.

After see my memories in a showcase
I started to understand the catharsis.

This is a colonizer language owning my wisdom as my
culture wasn't enough.

But is the goodness what makes my trip honest so I will
not celebrate towers on fire. I will not.

I've evolved to a self knowledge state that is
transforming itself every sunrise.

Since then,
I consider fasting as a window to settle.
I apologize for someone that is no me no more.

And then,
 I recite a rosary, faithless.
With the beads slipping over my undocumented scars.

PART I

PART II

1. Resilience
2. My tution fee was declined, twice

Interlude

3. Sunflower

Interlude

4. I love the weather
5. Last poem

GRACIAS

Printed in Great Britain
by Amazon

79999326R00021